E
Oan

Oana, Kay D.
The Little dog who wouldn't
be

DATE DUE		
MY 2 '84	APR 29 1986	APR 12 1
NOV 14	FEB 7 19	OCT 9 1991
APR 8	OCT 16 19	
MAY 7		APR 0 6 1993
SEP 1	OCT 18 19	APR 1 3 1993
OCT 17 1985	JAN 10 1990	OCT 2 3 1994
NOV 6	MAR 29 1990	
NOV 15	FEB 5 1994	SEP 1 4 1995
NOV 1 0 1991	MAR 16 1994	SEP 1 7 1995
JAN 4 1992	SEP 26 1990	
MAY 1 0 1988	OCT 5 1994	
SEP 2 1 1990		
OCT 3 19	MAR 27 19	

MEDIALOG
Alexandria, Ky 41001

THE LITTLE DOG
WHO WOULDN'T BE

illustrated by
Robert Russo

written by
Kay D. Oana

RAINBOW BOOKS

CARLSTADT, N. J.

First Rainbow Printing 1978

Library of Congress Catalog Card Number 77-18351

ISBN Number 0-89508-067-2

Printed in the United States of America.

Bruno was a plain brown dog. He was an ordinary dog with plain eyes and plain ears. Bruno even had a plain brown face.

Bruno didn't like being plain. He didn't like being brown. There were days when he didn't even like being a dog. He didn't like being a plain dog. Most of all, he just didn't like being a plain brown dog.

Bruno lived on a large, comfortable farm with Missy and Lonnie. Missy was the little girl who lived in the large white house with a fence around the yard. Missy was nice enough except she liked to play with kittens. Missy spent most of her time with kittens. She played with them, cuddled them, and held them.

Lonnie, her older brother, didn't play with kittens the way Missy did. He liked dogs. He especially liked Bruno. Since Lonnie liked Bruno, he didn't think Bruno was plain. Lonnie liked Bruno just as he was.

Bruno lived in the barn where it smelled of new-mown hay, and horses. He liked the barn.

But Bruno was unhappy as a dog. He was unhappy being a plain brown dog.

One night Bruno sat brooding in his corner of the barn. "I don't like being a dog. I don't like being a plain brown dog. If only I could be something else, then I would be happy."

He wandered outside and watched the moon come up over the barn. He told the moon how unhappy he was by howling. He howled as if his heart would break.

"I don't like being a dog. I don't like being a plain brown dog. If only I could be something else, then I would be happy."

In a nearby tree sat the ancient I-Know-Owl. The I-Know-Owl was thinking with his eyes closed. The I-Know-Owl spent most of his time with his eyes closed. The I-Know-Owl spent most of his time thinking.

The I-Know-Owl opened his large, deep, mysterious eyes and asked Bruno, "And just why are you so unhappy?"

Bruno wailed, "I don't like being a dog. I don't like being a plain brown dog." Tears rolled down his plain brown face. "If only I could be something else, then I would be happy."

"And just what do you think you would like to be?" asked the I-Know-Owl.

Bruno stopped howling and thought. "I think I would like to be something white. Let's see. A white rabbit! That's it! It would be fun to be a white rabbit. Everyone likes white rabbits."

The I-Know-Owl told Bruno, "Close your eyes and go to sleep. In the morning you will be a white rabbit."

Bruno went to sleep. The I-Know-Owl blinked his large, deep, mysterious eyes three times.

In the morning **Bruno** awakened to find himself a white rabbit. "How nice to be a white rabbit with soft fur and a bouncy, soft tail! Everyone likes white rabbits," Bruno told himself as he raced happily across the fields.

As Bruno raced across the fields, a large hunting dog began chasing him.

"Don't chase me!" Bruno yelped at the hunting dog. "Can't you see I'm just a plain, ordinary brown dog?"

Bruno remembered that he had been unhappy as a plain, ordinary brown dog. He was now a white rabbit.

Bruno ran and ran. Bruno tried to outrace the hunting dog, but the hunting dog was gaining.

Some workmen nearby were fitting round pipes into a draining ditch. Bruno ran for the ditch. He slipped into one of the round pipes.

The hunting dog followed him into the ditch. He put his long, pointed nose into the pipe but he just didn't fit. Bruno was safe from the hunting dog.

His heart pounded. "I'll stay in here until dark. Then the hunting dog will be gone," said Bruno to himself.

Bruno didn't notice that the workmen placed a heavy object at the entrance. The pipe where Bruno entered was now closed!

Bruno ran in the other direction. He ran through miles of pipes. Finally Bruno saw a glimmer of light in the distance. He kept running toward the light.

At last Bruno was out in the open air once again. He saw the stars winking at him in the sky. He said, "I must get back home to my barn."

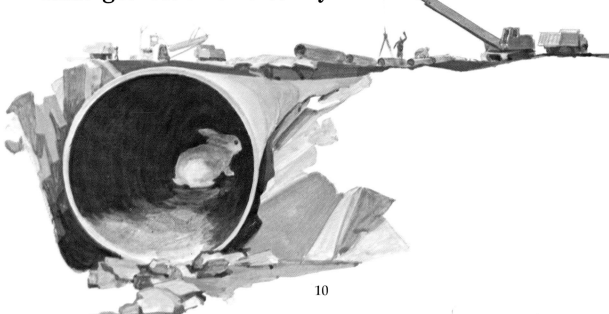

Bruno raced across the fields. It was still a long way from home. "Perhaps I could cross the road and get there faster," he thought.

As Bruno crossed the road, two huge beams of light shone down on him. A truck! He had not seen the truck coming. In passing over him, the big rubber tires roared on either side of him. The tires missed Bruno. His life was spared!

Back at the barn Bruno sobbed and sobbed.

The I-Know-Owl opened his large, deep, mysterious eyes. "I know. I know. You are unhappy as a white rabbit."

"But wait till I tell you. Three terrible things happened to me as a white rabbit. A hunting dog chased me, I was lost in a sewer, and a big truck ran over me!" Bruno blurted out.

"I know, I know," the I-Know-Owl repeated.

"Why didn't I know this before?" Bruno cried. "I thought I would be happy as a white rabbit. Why didn't I know this before?" he wailed.

When Bruno stopped sobbing he told the I-Know-Owl, "I think I would like to be something else. I think I would like to be a bird. Let's see. A red bird! That's it! It would be fun to be a red bird. Everyone likes red birds."

The I-Know-Owl told Bruno, "Close your eyes and go to sleep. In the morning you will be a red bird."

Bruno went to sleep. The I-Know-Owl blinked his large, deep, mysterious eyes three times.

In the morning Bruno awakened to find himself a red bird.

"How nice to be a red bird with bright red feathers and wings that fly! Everyone likes red birds," Bruno told himself as he strutted around the barnyard. He was proud of his bright red feathers.

One of Missy's kittens spotted the red bird. How large the kitten looked to Bruno!

Bruno cried, "Don't chase me! I'm just a plain, ordinary brown dog."

Bruno remembered that he had been unhappy as a plain, ordinary brown dog. He was now a red bird.

Bruno ran and ran. He tried to outrace the kitten, but the kitten's claws were getting closer. The kitten was gaining. Then he remembered he had wings and that he could fly. Just as the kitten was ready to pounce on him Bruno soared into the blue sky. He flew higher and higher. Bruno kept flying until he could no longer see the barn.

Suddenly he heard shots. Somebody was shooting!
Somebody was shooting at him! Bruno remembered.
Hunters do shoot at birds.

Bruno was terrified! Where could he hide? He
spotted a chimney. Bruno flew straight for the
chimney. He would be safe in the chimney!

Bruno reached the chimney and flew inside. But
there was no place to rest inside the chimney. Bruno
kept tumbling and tumbling. Down, down, down he
tumbled.

He finally landed in a pile of soft, sooty ashes. Bruno was covered with ashes from bill to tail. The ashes scattered like a cloud around him. Bruno sneezed and sneezed!

Bruno couldn't stay there in the cloud of ashes and sneeze forever. Maybe he could get out the way he came in. He flew up and up and up. Finally Bruno was out in the open air again.

He thought, "I must get back home to my barn." Bruno flew and flew across the fields. It was such a long way home.

Back at the barn Bruno cried and cried. Big tears rolled down his face again.

The I-Know-Owl opened his large, deep, mysterious eyes. "I know. I know. You are unhappy as a red bird."

"But wait till I tell you. Three terrible things happened to me as a red bird. I was chased by a cat, a hunter shot at me, and I tumbled down a chimney!" Bruno blurted out.

"I know, I know," the I-Know-Owl repeated.

"Why didn't I know this before?" Bruno cried. "I thought I would be happy as a red bird. Why didn't I know this before?" Bruno wailed.

When Bruno stopped crying he told the I-Know-Owl, "I think I would like to be something else. I think I would like to be a kitten. Let's see. A yellow kitten! That's it! It would be fun to be a yellow kitten. Everyone likes yellow kittens."

The I-Know-Owl told Bruno, "Close your eyes and go to sleep. In the morning you will be a yellow kitten."

Bruno went to sleep. The I-Know-Owl blinked his large, deep, mysterious eyes three times.

In the morning Bruno awakened to find himself a yellow kitten.

"How nice to be a yellow kitten — a fuzzy, cuddly, yellow kitten! Everyone likes yellow kittens," Bruno told himself as he stalked around the barnyard. He was proud of his soft, fuzzy, yellow fur.

Bruno walked with his head high, just the way he had seen Missy's kittens do.

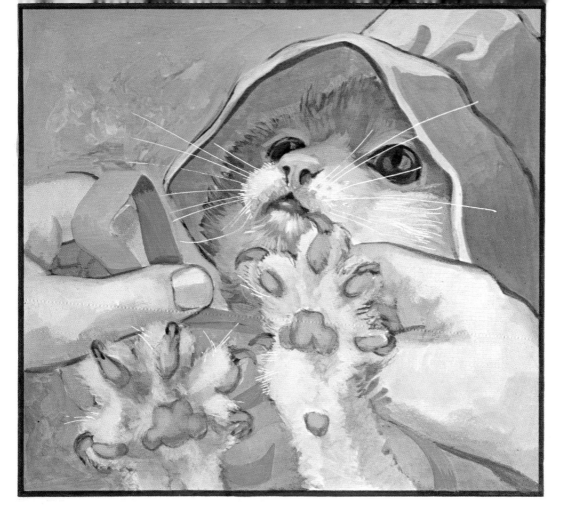

Missy spotted Bruno. "What a sweet, yellow, cuddly kitten. You must come and play with me."

Missy scooped Bruno up into her arms and ran back to the farmhouse. She placed a blue, starched bonnet on Bruno's head. She tied the bonnet strings under his chin.

Bruno wiggled and wiggled under the bonnet. He said, "Don't dress me up! I'm just a plain, ordinary brown dog."

Bruno remembered that he had been unhappy as a plain, ordinary brown dog. He was now a yellow, cuddly kitten.

Missy placed Bruno in a wicker buggy. She covered him with a pink blanket and started down the lane. This was the biggest insult of all! What if Bruno's friends saw him! Indeed! Bruno dressed up as a baby!

Bruno cried, meowed and scratched. He tried to jump out of the baby buggy.

Missy became angry with her new pet. She yanked the bonnet off and swatted Bruno with it. She said, "You are a bad cat. I don't want to play house with you."

Bruno ran and ran. He ran right into the milk shed and into a shiny, cool-looking can.

Bruno did not know the shiny can was filled with cream! He was soaked to his skin in thick, white cream! Bruno scrambled up the side of the milk can and ran as fast as he could. Bruno ran right up the big telephone pole. That would be a good place to dry out.

When he was at the top of the telephone pole, he sighed. Now he was safe from Missy and from silly baby bonnets. He could dry out from the thick, white cream. But when Bruno looked down he became frightened. He was so far up in the sky. How would he ever get down?

Bruno meowed and meowed and meowed. But no one paid attention to him down below. Darkness came and Bruno was still at the top of the telephone pole! He meowed louder and louder.

"Meow, MEOW, M - E - E - O - O - W!"

A neighboring farmer heard the cries. He brought a long, long ladder and climbed up the telephone pole. When he reached Bruno, the farmer carried him down.

On the ground the farmer swatted Bruno's tail. "And how do you expect us to get any sleep with you making all that noise?" the farmer scolded Bruno. The farmer swatted Bruno once more and said, "And don't try that again!"

Bruno was forlorn. "I must get back to my barn." Bruno ran and ran across the fields. It was such a long way home!

Back at the barn Bruno meowed and meowed some more.

The I-Know-Owl opened his large, deep, mysterious eyes. "I know. I know. You are unhappy as a yellow kitten."

"But wait until I tell you. Three terrible things happened to me as a yellow kitten. I was dressed up as a baby, I fell into a can of thick, white cream, and I was stranded on top of a telephone pole," Bruno blurted out.

"I know, I know," the I-Know-Owl repeated.

"Why didn't I know this before?" Bruno cried. "I thought I would be happy as a yellow kitten. Why didn't I know this before?" Bruno wailed. Big tears rolled down his face.

When Bruno stopped meowing he told the I-Know-Owl, "It's never as nice as it seems. I thought I would be happy being something else."

"I know, I know," the I-Know-Owl repeated.

"It wasn't so bad being a plain, ordinary brown dog. Why didn't I know this before?" Bruno howled.

The I-Know-Owl told Bruno, "Close your eyes and go to sleep. In the morning you will be a plain, ordinary brown dog."

"It's never as nice as it seems. It's never as nice as it seems," Bruno thought as he went to sleep.

The I-Know-Owl blinked his large, deep, mysterious eyes three times.

"I know, I know," the I-Know-Owl repeated.